PowerKiDS Readers

THE UNIVERSE
EL UNIVERSO

THE PLANETS

LOS PLANETAS

Elisa Peters

Traducción al español: Eduardo Alamán

PowerKiDS press.

New York

Published in 2013 by The Rosen Publishing Group, Inc.
29 East 21st Street, New York, NY 10010

First Edition

Editor: Amelie von Zumbusch
Book Design: Kate Laczynski

Traducción al español: Eduardo Alamán

Photo Credits: Cover iStockphoto/Thinkstock; pp. 4, 6, 20, 22, 24 (planet, sun) Shutterstock.com; pp. 8, 16, 18, 24 (rings) NASA/Handout/Getty Images News/Getty Images; p. 10 © PhotoDisc Imaging; p. 12 Jupiterimages/Comstock/Thinkstock; p. 14 Getty ESA/Handout/Images News/Getty Images.

Library of Congress Cataloging-in-Publication Data

Peters, Elisa.
[Planets. English & Spanish]
The planets = Los planetas / by Elisa Peters; [translated by Eduardo Alamán]. — 1st ed.
p. cm. — (Powerkids readers: the universe / el universo)
Includes index.
ISBN 978-1-4488-7825-3 (library binding)
1. Planets—Juvenile literature. 2. Solar system—Juvenile literature. I. Title. II. Title: Planetas.
QB602.P4518 2013
523.4—dc23

2011049991

Websites: Due to the changing nature of Internet links, PowerKids Press has developed an online list of websites related to the subject of this book. This site is updated regularly. Please use this link to access the list:
www.powerkidslinks.com/pkrtu/planets/

Manufactured in the United States of America

CPSIA Compliance Information: Batch #CS12PK: For Further Information contact Rosen Publishing, New York, New York at 1-800-237-9932

CONTENTS

CONTENIDO

The Sun is a **star**.

El Sol es una **estrella**.

Sun
El Sol
Mercury
Mercurio
Venus
Venus
Earth
Tierra
Mars
Marte
Jupiter
Júpiter
Uranus
Urano
Saturn
Saturno
Neptune
Neptuno

Eight **planets** circle it.

Ocho **planetas** giran alrededor del Sol.

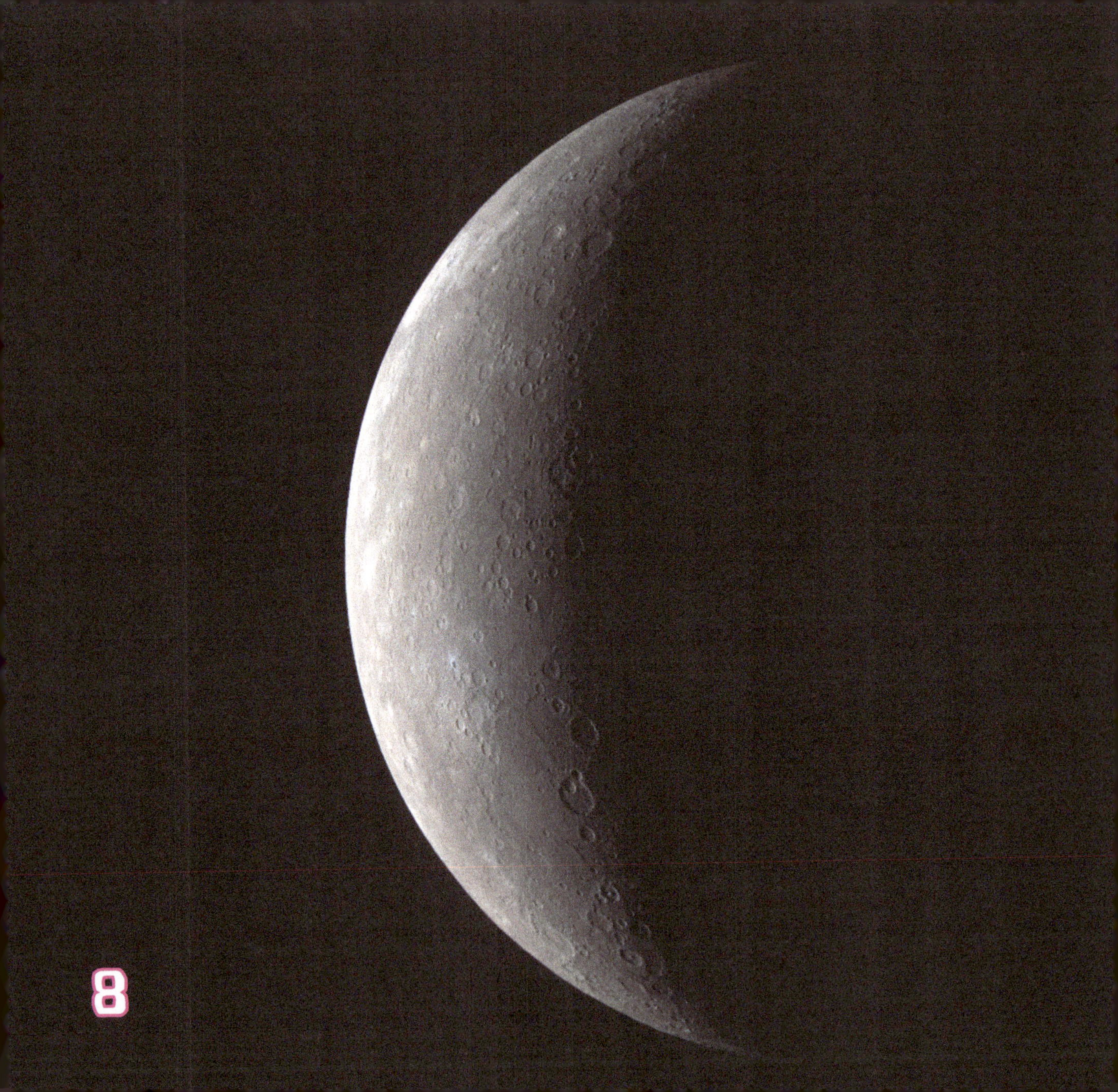

Mercury is the smallest.

Mercurio es el más pequeño.

Thick clouds cover Venus.

Venus está cubierto por nubes densas.

People live on Earth.

Nosotros vivimos en la Tierra.

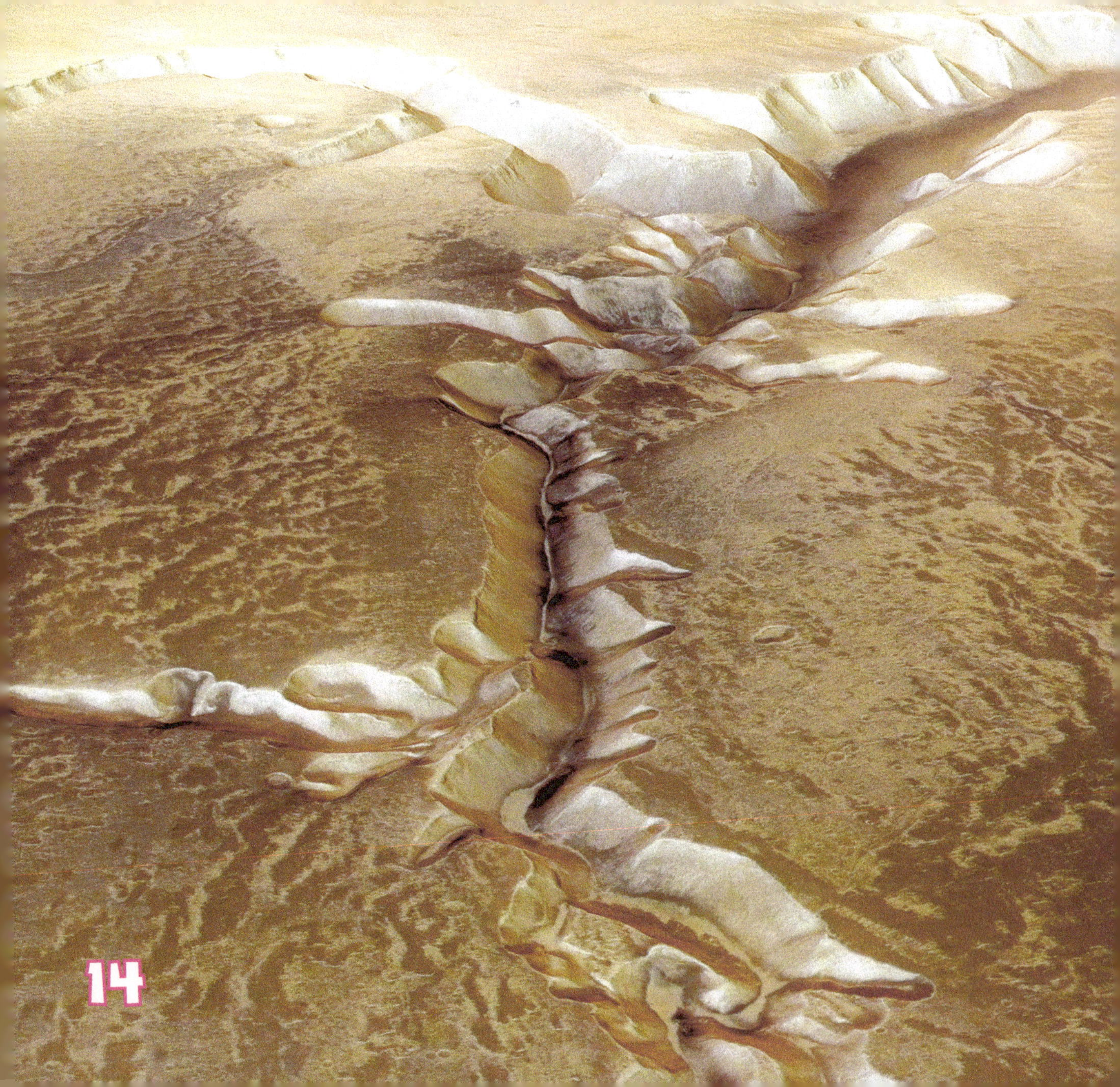

Mars is made of rock.

Marte está formado de rocas.

Jupiter is the biggest planet.

Júpiter es el planeta
más grande.

Saturn has many **rings** and moons.

Saturno tiene muchas lunas y **anillos**.

Uranus is made of gas.

Urano está formado de gas.

Neptune has the strongest winds.

Neptuno tiene vientos muy fuertes.

WORDS TO KNOW / PALABRAS QUE DEBES SABER

planets / (los) planetas

rings / (los) anillos

Sun / (el) Sol

INDEX

ÍNDICE